PIPING ME HOME

FRANKIE BLODGETT

authorHOUSE®

AuthorHouse™ LLC
1663 Liberty Drive
Bloomington, IN 47403
www.authorhouse.com
Phone: 1-800-839-8640

Published by AuthorHouse 07/26/2014

ISBN: 978-1-4969-2926-6 (sc)
ISBN: 978-1-4969-2925-9 (hc)
ISBN: 978-1-4969-2927-3 (e)

Library of Congress Control Number: 2014913185

This book is dedicated to my wife, Judith Blodgett
for all of her understanding and patience while
I was working on this book. She even added
this poem of her own: 'MY DACHSHUND'.

TABLE OF CONTENTS

CHAPTER 3

CHAPTER FOUR

CHAPTER NINE

MY DACHSHUND

Four legged little Wiener dog
You stand above the rest;
My loyal little comrade,
You truly are the best.

Precious little Wiener dog,
How you love to play;
The joy you give is endless
Each and every day.

Curious little Wiener dog
You are so very smart,
Full of love and kisses,
You are the captor of my heart!

Judith Blodgett

ACKNOWLEDGMENTS

Steven Earl for his friendship, support and wonderful photographs!

My grandson, Nicolas Bass for his assistance with the knowledge necessary to place this book on line for submission

INTRODUCTION

It is an extremely long trek from 1944 till 2014. This book is a poetic journey, of my life, from my birth until I'm 'PIPED HOME'. I was born to a railroad family in the small town of Chenango Forks, N. Y. My first two loves, the railroad and the Chenango River, ruled my life throughout my youth. Then we moved to Florida. To the 'SALT LIFE'. Atlantic fishing, boating and marine life studying became my interests. My favorite pastime was motoring out into the sea, out of sight of land. There I'd just drift and fish with only the sea, sky and GOD! The real story of my life lies with my unchanging love of GOD and AMERICA! Her forests, seas, rivers, lakes, mountains and golden plains are the world's best! The AMERICA of my youth, small town AMERICA, flag waving AMERICA!

CHAPTER 1

POEMS OF MY YOUTH

RAILROAD MEMORIES

I recall the smell of creosote
Emanating from the railroad ties;
With the mingling whiff of steam and smoke,
As the ole steam engine chugged on by.

The sound of its lonesome whistle,
Wailing out a hobo tune, which
Sticks in my soul like a thistle;
Tears at my heart as a wound.

The shimmering mirage of a ghostly train,
A spirit which transcends all time;
The memory of its spell ne'er wanes,
An image etched eternally in my mind.

The clickity-clack of the railway tracks
As the cars pass o'er each seam;
Still lures my mind, forever back,
To a life reminiscent of a dream.

So lay me down near the railway tracks;
Forever I'll hear that ole whistle wail.
My spirit will rise to each clickity-clack
And each passing train: I shall hail!!!

Frankie Blodgett

RAILROAD WARNING

On the rail
Western mail
Right on time
All is fine.

At a crossing
Rails blocking
'W' showing
Whistle blowing.

Sounding 'Q'
Loud and true
Before the crash
One last blast

MY CHENANGO

Living along the Chenango,
A riparian delight;
Her eternal flowing waters,
Fueled my propensity for life.

Her quaint old bridges and trestles,
Graciously reflect a bygone era;
An age when life moved lazily;
At times, seemingly without a care.

My childhood on the Chenango,
Reminiscent of 'Tom and Huck's',
Complete with rafts and fishing;
I wouldn't trade it for a million bucks.

Frankie Blodgett

The hours spent screening for Dobson
Or chasing crayfish 'round the rocks';
Diving into the ole swimming hole
Fishing from bridges, shore and docks.

Once there existed an old canal,
A small stretch could still be found,
Complete with a lock and towpath,
At 'The Forks', just north of town.

The green algae filled water,
Teemed with aquatic life,
Turtles, newts and pollywogs;
Truly a young boy's delight.

However, that was o'er fifty years ago;
Life has relocated me far away;
My mind oft wanders lovingly back
To her banks, even yet today.

One day soon, I plan to return
When my days are at their end;
My spirit will recapture the felicity
Of my dear Chenango once again.

CHAPTER 2

NATURE

NATURES KINGDOM

Where the endless water is the sea,
A salty mariner, there shall be,
Ever adrift on the foamy brine,
Sailing forever; till the end of time.

Where the earth becomes the vast blue sky
A fearless aviator there shall fly,
Soaring freely among the clouds,
High above the maddening crowds.

Where the wilderness escapes the town,
A brave adventurer shall be found,
Scouting out Gods wild frontier,
Living freely amongst bear and deer.

Where the soul meets with boundless freedom,
That will be in: 'NATURES KINGDOM'
Eternally free to roam, sail and soar:
A brave spirit free for ever more!

Frankie Blodgett

HIKE ON A MOONLESS NIGHT

Adventuring a hike on a moonless night,
Can take your senses to incredible heights;
Earthly features are of little value,
Nothing recognizable can you follow.

Haunts and shadows line your travel;
With bearings lost, your wits unravel;
Don't panic as a helpless dove;
Just turn your eyes to the stars above.

Merak and Dubhe point the way.
Ensuring from your course, you'll never stray;
But avoid getting lost in the dragon's tail,
For Polaris can appear somewhat pale.

Knowledge of the heavens is the key,
To keep your mind ever worry free;
So if you hike on a moonless night,
Always keep the stars within your sight.

NOT SO SILENT

The silence of a sylvan eve,
A fallacy believed by most;
Yet in weather fair or stormy,
Peal forth sounds t'would scare a ghost.

The eerie hoot of an ole owl,
Silhouetted against the moon;
From its perch high in a long leaf pine;
Blares out its ever spectral tune.

The bellowing of a bull frog,
As it echoes from a pristine pond;
This Rena's deep resonant croak,
Booms thru the forest and beyond.

The blatting of the nighthawk,
As it darts about in flight;
It's deafening bull-batic blasts,
Rock the silence of the night.

The male droning of the cicada,
From the surrounding trees and thickets;
Accompanied with a background chorus,
Of peepers, cooing dove and crickets.

When the night sky's lit by lightning;
With the thunders rumbling roar:
Even the world's greatest composers,
Could never equal such a score!

Frankie Blodgett

SOUNDS OF NATURE

A gentle breeze murmurs as on wings,
Softly sighing as it maunders along;
Upon a porch a wind chime sings,
Natures soothing harmonic song.

The distant call of a waterfall,
As it cascades down a mountain side;
With the thunderous roar from the canyon floor,
As the wild waters with rocks collide.

The soft purl of a peaceful rill,
As it meanders lost in time,
Trickles softly down a gentle hill;
Whispering out an age old rhyme.

The euphoric murmur of the doves coo,
Serenely warbles throughout the wood,
Instantly removing all the city blues,
As well as anything in Nature could.

The soft tap of the gentle rain,
As it greets the leafy forest floor;
Till the mighty wind takes the reins;
The rain drives and the thunder roars.

May Natures thunder eternally roll?
And the ground dove forever coo;
Then future generations will e'er know;
The glorious sounds of Nature: that we knew!

DUSK

Dusk, the Omega, the end of day,
When shadows dance in the suns last ray;
Twilight deepens into its darkest hue
And the night birds sing, as if on cue.

Hungry bats swoop in the dusky sky;
The nightingale sings his lullaby;
A morph begins in the diurnal world;
The nocturnal realm has now unfurled.

In the gloom of this darkened time,
My fretting mind oft begins to pine
O'er the raison d'etre of my being
And if I'm grasping life's true meaning.

Yet, the slow dance of the fading light
Doth ease the gloaming into night;
Joyously, I'm sure, when night is done,
A new day dawns with the rising sun!

Frankie Blodgett

DAWN

Dawn, the Genesis, the beginning of day
An earthly juvenescence, a constant replay;
The suns golden rays, Gods outstretched hands
Bring an exhilarating rebirth over the land.

A heralding glow in the eastern sky
Assures a sleepy world that day is nigh;
The radiant stars in their dark realm above
Are quickened away by the morning sun.

As above the horizon the sun doth peek;
The world awakens from a lifeless sleep;
With the rays of light setting the world aglow
Yet, it's the timeless sun that steals the show.

A rising blue mist o'er an emerald sea
From the conquering sun doth rapidly flee;
Ole' Sols reflection on the shimmering swells;
From the shadows of night, my fear is quelled.

FORT CLINCH

At the north end of Amelia,
Where the waters of three rivers blend,
Lies Florida's best kept secret,
As a vacation spot, a ten.

Where the blue Atlantic waters
Kiss Amelia's silver sands,
An Eden so uniquely designed;
Truly the work of God's great hands.

Where stands of golden sea oats
Wave cheerfully to the sea,
From peaceful rolling sand dunes;
A view, so wild, so free.

Where golden rays of sunlight
Pierce the grand canopy above,
Illuminating the morning mist;
As if a spotlight of God's love.

Where in glorious vivid sunsets,
Your dreamy eyes catch a world aglow;
While capturing an outbound trawler,
On Amelia's pristine tidal flow

This euphoric destination,
This truly wondrous landmark;
Fort Clinch, as she's referred to,
Is the gem of Florida Parks!

FORT CLINCH (DESCRIPTIVE)

At the north end of Amelia
Where the waters of three rivers blend,
Lies Florida's best kept secret,
As a vacation spot, a ten.

Where the blue Atlantic Waters
Kiss Amelia's silver sands,
An Eden so uniquely designed,
Truly the work of God's great hands.

Where stands of golden sea oats
Wave cheerfully to the sea
From peaceful rolling sand dunes,
A view; so wild, so free!

Where golden rays of sunlight
Pierce the grand canopy above,
Illuminating the morning mist
As a spotlight of God's love.

This euphoric destination,
This truly wondrous land mark;
Fort Clinch as she's
Is the gem of Florida Parks!

Silhouetted against the morning sky
Boldly stands the namesake of the park
Fort Clinch in all her historic splendor,
A glorious adventure to embark.

With her cannons pointed seaward,
Reenactors filling every post,
The eighteen-sixties come alive
In the jewel of Florida's coast.

Your mind slips back in history,
Then your eyes, you begin to rub
For behind a sentry on the wall
Passes a nuclear-powered sub.

The sub will pass a fishing pier,
One of the grandest in the nation;
A picturesque observation point
And awesome fishing destination.

The park has two popular campgrounds,
Each as different as night and day;
Both with extraordinary qualities,
Each designed in their own unique way.

Nestled below an oaken canopy
With a peaceful view of the sound,
Each site buffered with sabal palms;
Rests the cozy River Campground.

Where groups gather 'round their fires,
While tasty camp foods are prepared,
The joy of smoors or marshmallows
With friends and family shared.

Where in glorious vivid sunsets
Your dreamy eyes catch a world aglow,
While capturing an outbound trawler
On Amelia's pristine tidal flow.

In stark contrast, in brilliant sun
The Beach Campground views an aqua sea,
With spacious sites, under starry skies;
Your spirit becomes so alive and free.

You may stroll down to the water,
Feel the east wind in your face,
Take a deep breath of pure sea air,
Feel your excited heart begin to race.

Frankie Blodgett

Gently place your towel upon the sand
Lie in Florida's tanning rays;
Then have an exhilarating swim
In the Atlantic's cooling waves.

While on the beach, try shelling
You can collect them by the pail;
While for the bikers and the hikers
There are miles of roads and trails.

Visit the picnic area and playground,
The grand museum and gift shop;
Then tour old Fernandina,
For out the gate it's just a hop.

This quaint historic village
Will make your trip complete;
When taking in its Shrimp Festival
And the blessing of the fleet.

So when traveling down to Florida
Your trip will be a sensation;
If you make ole Fort Clinch
Your vacation destination.

A DAY IN HEAVEN

I ventured out for a peaceful drive;
I must have crashed, I must have died;
For I found myself at heaven's gate;
The streets of gold were colored slate.

No host of angels, did I see;
A uniformed sentry greeted me;
He waved me in and smiled hello;
He had no wings and no halo.

Lining the streets was glorious greenery,
Huge pine trees, majestic scenery;
Turkey and deer roamed at leisure;
Scurrying squirrels took a breather.

The rare fox squirrel made an appearance
Free to live without interference;
Pocket gophers lived under mounds,
Seldom appearing above the ground.

I came upon cabins and great campgrounds
With joyous campers all around
Soon I arrived at a picnic area;
People there were even merrier.

The entire scene gave me a thrill;
Happy families around their grills
Dads grilling up their steaks,
Children swimming in the lake.

People jogging, people biking,
People canoeing, people hiking;
Everyone enjoying life with a passion;
This was the heaven, I'd imagined!

Suddenly I crashed back to reality;
I hadn't become a fatality;
I hadn't crashed, I hadn't died,
I hadn't passed to the other side.

I had entered a heaven on Earth;
My soul had undergone rebirth:
But the time was late and growing dark;
So I had to leave GOLD HEAD BRANCH STATE PARK!

TRIBUTE TO THE LONG LEAF PINE

God blessed the Earth with evergreens,
The long leaf pine surpassed his dreams,
The noblest of the southern pines,
The most remarkable of its kind.

With maturity their tops do bend,
As if looking down with scorn toward men;
The sorrow expressed in each cat face;
The scars which time can ne'er erase.

Frankie Blodgett

Some have endured for hundreds of years;
Each tree lost, should bring man's tears;
In the elder of trees, their canopy's flat,
As if a throne on which God sat.

Venerable trees dropped where they stood;
For man's insatiable desire for wood;
Their population constantly tumbling,
Due to indiscriminate lumbering.

Oh! Will the logging ever stop?
As did the turpentiner's pots;
The injustice of each logger's blade
Has turned grand forests into glades.

May this majestic tree, stand in peace;
With each New Year, her seeds release;
Ensuring there shall forever be:
God's gift to man: this glorious tree!

COCKADED

Above the old cat face
In a long leaf's sturdy bole
Exists a little aperture
A long endeavored hole.

Hear the tireless tapping,
See the sticky resin ooze,
Notice the small picinae,
Watch in awe and muse.

A unique little woodpecker,
For it dwells in a living pine,
Apart from other species,
Distinct trait of its kind.

Its plume is not remarkable
A peppered black and white;
A little red on the males head,
Seems to suit this bird just right.

When predators come a-callin'
They face a formidable task,
Making it through the gooey mess
Which is the pine tree's sap.

But lumbering and development
Have depleted its habitat,
Now listed on the endangered list;
Hopefully, its numbers will come back!

Frankie Blodgett

PURE MOUNTAINS STILL

From piedmont to pinnacle, earth to sky;
From the morning mist to the birds that fly;
From the green flowered glens to the tarns of blue;
The mountains tantalize the senses with their view.

Of poetry and song, the mountains e'er ring,
For the 'Muses of Parnassus' still do sing.
The glorious alpenglow still greets the eye;
And the slopes are still teemin' with butterflies.

From humble monticules up to noble peaks;
Of lofty grandeur of which poets speak;
Of grazing ibex and big horn sheep
On green and flowery versants, e'er so steep.

The grand cascading of water, o'er a precipice,
The majesty as it plummets is tough to resist,
For the mountains are 'Mother Nature', at her best
Its adventure and enchantment, the end of your quest!

COLONNADE OF SERENITY

I came upon a forest,
Like a fortress on the plains;
A timeless colonnade of nature;
A harboring refuge from life's strain.

Dancing shadows beckoned to me
As the outstretched hand of God;
Was this truly a mystic place?
Or a mind conceived mirage.

Inside guided rays from heaven,
Pierced through the canopy above,
Illuminating the forest floor,
Spotlighting a fleeing pair of dove.

The enchantment of this ageless wood;
This divinely inspired scene;
The wonder and the beauty of which
Could only be found in dreams.

Against the wooded background,
A cautious buck slowly raised his head;
While a busy robin gathered worms,
Making sure her chicks were fed.

The wonder of the moment
With an owls mesmerizing call;
Drew me ever closer to
The serenity of it all.

Frankie Blodgett

UNDERSTANDING NATURE

I sit here before this naked window,
Fixed eyes engaging a sad ole willow;
With gaze enthralled, mind disconnected;
A thousand times o'er, this tree inspected.

Yet, seeing only bark and leaves;
Not the essence which is the tree.
My purblind mind sadly recognizes not,
That in nature which my heart has sought.

I sit, pen in hand, at my oaken desk,
A blind heart beating within my chest,
A blank sheet of paper before me lies;
Why am I unable to recognize?

Nature is understood through enlightened perception;
Ne'er limited to scholarly erudition.
So as down life's natural path, I trod;
I've now discovered the eminence of: NATURES GOD!!

CHAPTER 3

THE SEA

FREE AT SEA

To be adrift on the endless sea
Is the only place my soul is free;
No land in sight nor ships nor men,
The sea and sky are my only friends.

Away from the problems, sin and crime,
Afloat in a bubble, lost in time;
Lost in a world that has no bounds,
As if floating among the cotton clouds.

Only GOD, could create such a freedom
Which sets my tingling senses reeling;
The peace and serenity, that dost surround,
Is seldom ever elsewhere found.

Frankie Blodgett

LIFE'S BIG QUESTION

To work or fish
That is the question
And one that
Always shall be.

To pay the bills
One must work
Yet to fish
You're truly free!

THE SIREN TRIALS

Seamen know
What lies below
The blue and tranquil sea.
The Gods of time
Can't solve the rhyme
Of what keeps their spirits free.

The Sirens sing,
Their voices ring,
Many rush to doom;
Neptune sighs,
Poseidon cries,
These seamen died too soon.

That Leviathan devil
And Kraken revel
From their lairs down in the deep;
With failed test,
The seamen's bodies rest
In the locker of eternal sleep!

ETERNALLY DOOMED TO SAIL

We headed our trawler out to sea,
For a night of netting shrimp;
Six hours out, our eyes were stunned,
By that, which they had caught a glimpse.

Adrift upon the mystic sea,
In the new moons only light;
A relic of antiquity,
A vestige lost in time.

The slapping of relentless waves,
Against her timeworn hull;
The flapping of her torn old sails,
Draped from her masts, so tall.

Awash and barely afloat,
This derelict, shunned by the living,
Doomed to sail for ever more'
On a sea, so unforgiving.

Upon her decks, a ghostly crew;
A fearsome specter at the helm,
With blood and sweat upon his brow,
His eyes, shewn the fires of Hell.

For piracy and crimes a'sea,
The damnation of ship and crew,
The captives of tormenting winds,
'Twas from the depths of Hell, they blew.

Then, as quickly as she'd appeared,
This phantom suddenly vanished;
Her home the sea, for eternity;
From safe harbor, forever banished!

BATTLE ON THE JETTY

I need to tell you a fishing tale,
For the most part it is true,
Of the day I wrestled a doormat flounder;
Most likely, the actions of a fool.

I baited my hook with a plump mud minnow,
As lively as could be found;
Then I made my way o'er the slippery rocks,
Trying not to slip and drown.

I dropped my line, right next to the rocks
And within a minute or two,
The float went under, I set the hook;
It was a nice fish, I just knew.

Frankie Blodgett

Well the battle raged on for quite a while,
Till I pulled him from the sea;
But as I held it up, the fish flipped-off;
To my despair, once again he was free.

Without thinking twice or even once,
I dropped down to my knees
And grabbed his tail, but the slime prevailed;
His tail I was unable to seize.

He flopped along, among the rocks,
Trying to reach the sea;
I also flopped along, among the rocks,
Attempting to recapture the escapee.

We rolled around, among the rocks
With arms and fins a' flying,
The rocks and shells were taking their toll
But, defeat I was denying.

I came off those ragged rocks,
With more wounds than I could list;
With slime and blood all over me;
But, I had that dern ole fish!!

NATURES GUIDANCE

A heavy mist was rolling in
As I peered out ahead of me,
The moon was nearly hidden,
Little could I see?

For I was on a mission
But knew not, which way to tread,
If I should choose unwisely,
I would soon be dead.

So I stared out in bewilderment
Knowing not, which way to go,
When nature's voices summoned me;
Head for the silvery glow.

Filtered moonlight upon the water,
The mystic pull of the sea,
The slapping waves upon the sand
My course, now seemed clear to me.

So very slowly, I made my way,
Now as confident as could be;
This sea turtle hatchling felt relief,
As my tiny flippers, slipped into the sea!

BUCKING THE TIDE

We entered the port of Cay Resort,
'Twas no pilot at the wheel;
With shoals and rock, from sea to dock
And a jagged reef concealed.

We were in for a ride, a running ebb tide;
Would we have ample draft?
With waves beating and water receding;
Would we ground or would we waft?

There was no relaxing, as we were wafting,
O'er the nearing sandbar;
A slight little bump, no more of a thump;
The hull was uncompromised thus far.

And yet, we still shared dread, for up ahead,
Lie a very narrow strait,
Which ran above a reef, a cause for grief;
Any miscue would seal our fate.

A jagged rock, would surely put a stop,
To the voyage of any tall ship;
A wooden hull, the locker's call;
The sudden end to any trip.

The Captain was skilled and knowledge filled;
The helmsman a seasoned old salt;
The crew was steady and always ready,
To standoff any assault.

The winds were stable and very favorable;
Though we ran with a hostile tide;
We ran true, as we viewed,
The reef 'neath our lu'ard {leeward} side.

With nerves frayed and wharfage paid,
We lie at wharf, tightly moored;
With setting sun and voyage done:
We then, gave thanks unto the Lord!!

TRIBUTE TO THE LIGHT KEEPER

Frankie Blodgett

From the massive ledge light tower,
The old light keeper ever peers,
Dauntless in his steadfast watch,
O'er the sea, he so reveres.

Living in a mighty bastion,
A staunch fortress from rough seas;
He tends his lamp with deep devotion;
While his free spirit, rides the breeze.

Living a life of isolation;
Preforming mundane tasks,
Lugging oil up the stairs,
Polishing all the brass.

He faithfully toils, around the clock,
Fulfilling tasks which never end,
Such as, keeping the prisms adjusted and clean,
Of the lights intricate Fresnel lens.

Yet, being always ready,
To rescue ships and men;
Prepared to place his life in peril,
For those, he's sworn to defend.

A guardian over seamen,
Who voyage near his post;
A savior of all who wreck,
Along the harbor coast.

For the sea is extremely unpredictable;
A violent storm, may suddenly appear;
Thus the light must always be diligently manned,
By a courageous keeper, who knows, yet shows no fear!

NOT IN SEARCH OF BEAUTY

I waded out into the sound,
Cast net in hand and peering down;
A brilliant sun rising in the East,
The entire world seemed at peace.

The water was extremely clear,
Windless surface smooth as a mirror;
While at my feet grew saw grass stands,
Anchored in rippled white sea sands.

Ahead a cautious blue crab fled,
Disappearing into an oyster bed;
Playful porpoise, rose and dove,
All throughout the spacious cove.

A timid leatherback raised her head,
Chewing a jellyfish as she fled;
An ole mullet leaped from the blue,
With a hungry 'black tip' in pursuit.

Osprey, gulls and brown pelican,
Spanish moss and a cypress stand,
Enhance the beauty, around the sound,
For here the best of nature doth abound.

Oh! How easily my mind could stray
And save my duties for another day;
But I was not in search of beauty,
Sadly my day was filled with other duties.

Frankie Blodgett

KNOW THE SEA

Ahoy mate!
Scuttlebutt has it,
Ye claim to know the sea;
Such travesty!!
Avast these wayward notions,
Thar lead ye to the locker,
At the bottom of the ocean.

Listen mate!
Hear me out,
Change ye life is what it's all about;
Turn me a live ear mate,
Or ye will surely seal your fate;
Ye'll booze and rum it, all life long
And eagerly run to the siren songs.

Please mate!
Why can't ye see?
This land life, will bury thee;
Think not of the joys of man
Or of the evils of the land;
Be ye one with the rollin' sea,
Only then, will ye find victory.

Think mate!
Do not be a fool;
This is what ye need to do;
To truly receive the seas reward,
Turn ye face ever seaward;
Lean ye into the saline spindrift
And sail into the mystic mist.

Now mate!
The time's at hand,
For ye to stop and make your stand.
Float upon the salty brine,
Forever till the end of time;
Permit your soul to e'er roam;
Free your spirit on the rollin' foam.

Alas mate!
Success is here.
Hold your accomplishments, oh so dear!
You've done all this and now ye see,
That you've fulfilled your destiny.
Now ye can say and I'll agree,
That ye do truly know the sea!

TIME STANDS STILL
ON A PLACID SEA

Time stands still on a placid sea;
No worries, no cares and a mind that's free;
With fixed stare, my mind's a slave,
To a mesmerizing pattern of waves.

The mirrored sea, sparkles and shines,
In a heavenly manner, aye divine;
The washed-out sky in an ancient sleep,
No definitive border mark sky and deep.

In the light blue tint of the sea below,
The darting fish put on a splendid show;
While jellyfish in their medusa form,
Delicately float in the waters warm.

With an ole loggerhead in natural pursuit,
Unconcerned by the diving of a nearby coot;
Graceful seabirds wing above it all,
Filling the air with their familiar calls.

Where nature and trance blend into one,
A euphoric state excelled by none;
Having visited here, it's plain to me:
Time stands still on a placid sea!!

FIND YOUR DESTINY

Years ago, when I was young,
Many a song, my wild heart sung;
But the landly life had sickened me;
My soul was dead, my spirit unfree.

As I lie asleep upon the beach,
My goals in life seemed out of reach;
A mystic fog silently came ashore
And touched my soul for evermore.

I awoke to the foghorns alerting moan;
Thru the mystic mist, a faint moon shown;
The vapor particles danced about,
When from the fog, came a ghostly shout:

"Ahoy thar matey" was the call,
"Now's the time to spend it all,
The sea's the answer to yar woes,
Head ye outward t'where the trade winds blow.

Frankie Blodgett

A seaman on his ship a' sea;
Akin to a knight upon his steed;
The grandest sense of unity known;
A harmony which resonates to the bone.

The freedom of Gods rollin' seas,
Not unlike a feather upon a breeze;
Free to float where the soft winds blow;
Free to sail where the Gulf Stream flows."

The years have flown, I've grown frail,
No longer am I able to sail;
Oh! The tales I could tell of ships and ports,
Of steamy women and colorful cohorts.

I followed my dreams without regret;
Sailed the seas with no course set;
A thousand lives condensed into one;
An adventurous life, exceeded by none!

CALL OF THE SEA

Far beyond the horizon; out beyond my view;
A mystic voice summons me, as if a lover's woo:
Mother Earth is beckoning, from the deep blue sea;
As if calling a lost child home:" Please come unto me!"

She grabs like a hawk with her talons in the wind;
Her voice so like a 'Siren's song'; singing me on in.
Her emerald colored water is so purely refined,
It sparkles and it glistens in a manner divine.

My olfactory is struck by the fresh saline sea air;
Her soft blowing spindrift; leaves my soul without a
care;
The mesmerizing pattern of her e'er slapping waves,
Soothes my worried soul, while removing all of my rage.

The freedom of the open waters; the lure of the sea,
Grabs at my spirit; thus igniting a spark within me;
So as long as I'm allowed, to roam upon the Earth;
The choice to remain at sea: will always be my first!

BONES OF THE SEA

Many are born to a life a sea,
This hardy lot of men, they be;
Upon their ships, a courageous band;
Home at sea, shunning the land.

Taverns, pubs and alike can be found,
Adjacent to the wharves of every port town;
Sea stories bluster, from each new docker,
Tellin' of mates, who'd been summoned to the locker.

Summoned by duty, claimed by the sea;
Fulfilling an age old destiny;
Swept from their vessels, lost to their mates;
The challenge of the sea had sealed their fates.

Oh! The tales, the locker could tell,
Of mariners, sailors and fishermen as well,
Courageous souls who were swallowed by the sea;
Their now captive spirits, ne'er again free.

Their bones lie scattered, upon the bed
Eternally sleeping, souls undead;
There to remain until the end of time,
Far below the billowy brine.

Lying, yes; but ne'er silently;
E'er rattling! E'er violently!
The bones of the sea rattle, oh so loudly.
Of those who'd sailed, so very proudly!

THE PARALLEL

Listen, please me matey,
I'm here to set ye straight;
Ye course is far from steady,
So mind yer rudder mate.

The skies ahead are darkening;
The seas are rollin' tall;
Put yer nose upon a swell,
Do not let her rise and fall.

Keep yer eyes on the horizon'
Do not e'er let them blink;
For a moment of distraction,
Could cause yer ship to sink.

A souls trying path through life,
Parallels a ship a 'sea,
Both must heed all warning signs,
If a safe passage there is to be.

So in life, as well as sailin';
May both be peril free?
'May GOD always bless ye with
Fair winds and following seas'

Frankie Blodgett

MASTER WIND

A majestic nor'easter;
I, a curious seeker
Wandered down to the wild sea;
To a witches brew,
Neptune's deadly stew;
The dark side of her majesty.

The waves were beating;
The shoreline retreating,
Erosion was taking its toll;
With no sign of calming
It was somewhat alarming:
How far would this washout go?

The old fishing pier
Which has stood here for years
Was weakened and looked soon to collapse;
Yet the old pilings seemed strong
And might weather the storm:
Still be standing at storms end, perhaps.

Saline foam was a flying;
There was no denying
The wind was the master here;
While whipping up waves
The sea was its slave;
Spawning my admiration, as well as fear.

UNSEEN POWER

A nor'easter was a blowin'
On that cool November day;
The spindrift was a flyin';
The wind came whippin' off the bay.

The red morn had warned me
Of a gale movin'in;
The sea and all her fury
Driven by the mystic wind.

I peered ever seaward
As I leaned into the gale;
The wind was my master,
I felt so very frail.

I stared in vast be wonderment
T'ward a force I couldn't see;
How something this invisible
Could move the clouds and sea.

IN THE ARMS OF THE SEA

In the arms of the sea,
No safety be,
But at least your soul is free;
Yet, the roll of the swells,
As you know well,
Is soft when the wind is lee.

But when the wind's a gale,
It's without fail,
The sea sparks other tales,
Of brave seafaring souls,
As in yarns of old,
Felt the seas wrath when they sailed.

The waves and the breakers,
Accept all takers,
When Aeolus awakens 'la mere'
You'll need strength and courage,
To overcome the rue age,
If you are to persevere.

PEACE FROM ORIGIN

Adrift on the sea, my sanity saved,
Mind lost to a mesmerizing pattern of waves,
Inducing a trancelike peaceful condition;
My mind surrendered to this soothing rendition.

The seas meditative powers, immense;
A natural measure of wisdom dispensed,
With a measured degree of soft inner peace;
The anguish and misery, my soul doth release.

The mystical dance, of the rollin' swells,
Has once again, worked its magical spell;
My loosened spirit, now sings in the blue spindrift,
As the sacred sea pulled my heart e'er dear to it.

All life on Earth, evolved in the sea;
A sacred bond, there always shall be.
Man's spirit will always be pulled by the seas rise and fall
For Natures God is the creator of all!!!

A SAILORS VERSE

A glorious new dawn was burstin' forth,
O'er the horizon to the East,
With a grand array of brilliant shades,
Ranging from dark salmon to soft pink.

My eyes beheld its beauty,
Truly a sight to behold;
Yet down my back a shiver ran,
O'er the calamity it foretold.

A red sky in the morning,
Foretold of a rising breeze,
Which always is accompanied by
The roughening of the seas.

The glass was rapidly emptying
And the sea began to roll,
Leaving very little doubt,
Of that, which the sky foretold.

A nor'easter was upon us,
With its squalls and gale force blasts;
We had battened down our hatches,
Though we feared she wouldn't last.

Our bilges were taking water,
The well deck was totally awash;
The vessel was listing, steep to port;
The hulls integrity was also lost.

The safety of the harbor, lie before us;
However, we were buckin' a strong headwind;
Our ship was near dead in the water,
A battle our diesels couldn't win.

The gale raged on, throughout the day,
Ship and crew were taking a beating;
Then late afternoon, the wind swung about,
The sea began retreating.

We now ran with a lu'ard (leeward) wind,
While a flood tide greeted our keel;
As landfall welcomed our searching eyes,
We proceeded inshore with newfound zeal.

While high above, in the evening heavens,
A red sky had lighted our way;
The wisdom of a sailors verse,
Had proven true again today!

WITH THE POETS, I AGREE

Poets write of mesmerizing waves;
And of seamen, eternally crazed,
By the roaring surf, forever free,
Aye- the eternal pulse of the sea.

One glorious, bright and windless morn,
A pang of desire was suddenly born,
To sojourn down to the poetic sea;
To determine, if I, with the dreamers did agree.

I was totally stunned and swept with awe,
O'er the dazzling vision, which I saw;
For the indomitable spirit of Gods seas;
Instantly, loosened my heart and set it free.

Frankie Blodgett

The prism arcs of the rainbowed spray,
Beauteously appeared an amazing array;
While the mystic flight of the blown spume,
Frothed spiritedly from the breakers womb.

Yet, beyond the surf, rests a languid sea,
As tranquil as a sheltered lee;
An aqua sea, below a salmon sky,
Appeared as if stained with a heavenly dye.

The mirrored reflection of ole Sol,
Wondrously set the sea aglow;
While the rhythmic roll, of the perpetual swells;
Created a soothing hypnotic spell.

For spellbound, I shall forever be;
Succumbed to the seas shimmering majesty;
Exalt my heart! O'er this newly found wonder,
Which impels my heart, to beat as thunder!

Yes, poets write of mesmerizing waves,
The eternal pulse of the sea, men crave;
Beating infinitely upon the timeless seas,
And beating e'er deeper within the heart of me!!

SEA CURSE

This is an elegy of wrack and of ruin;
Of flotsam of scattered bodies and debris;
Of a captain defeated by merciless waves,
Swiftly generated by the winds stormy seas.

The Captain was a notorious seaman,
Greatly renowned to the ends of the Earth;
An intrepid, lion-hearted ship master;
A genuine 'Child of the Sea' from his birth.

He was doomed by his compulsive nature
And of his lifelong quest to conquer the sea;
Ultimately, the sea reigned victorious,
Yet from his obsession, he'd ne'er be free.

His mighty ship was as easily destroyed
As a sea foam bubble slapped by a reed;
His valiant crew claimed by the locker,
Lost victims of his cursed and constant breed.

Frankie Blodgett

Yet he clung to his ship like a remora
Or a barnacle attached to its hull
And thrillingly rode the tempestuous waves,
Completely ignoring death's ominous call.

It is said; when the winds of Hell rile the sea gods
And the full moon shines gold on the blue seas face,
Across the night sky, on a wild sea of clouds,
A ghostly ship doth desperately race.

At her helm, a crazed and brazen madman,
As through perdition, he eternally sails;
His damnation- to battle the timeless sea,
Conquest denied, evermore doomed to fail!

THE SPIRITS OF THE SPRAY

When the wild nor'easter turns gale force
Tempestuous waves are driven forth,
Raging waves producing far flung spray
Arc beauteously in the suns bright rays.

Within the blue aura of the mist
Silent entities do mystically exist,
Dancing joyously in the blown spume
To the timeless Sirens e'er enticing tunes.

The vapor pennant which is commonly seen
Is but a spindrift trail as they careen,
Vibrantly racing about on the blast,
Driving the spray e'er higher as they dash.

Wherever the wild winds kick up grand waves,
Like which send helpless surfers to their graves;
There can be found frantic spirits at play
For they are the eternal 'SPIRITS OF THE SPRAY".

Frankie Blodgett

CHAPTER FOUR

MY NAVY YEARS

CAN'T FLOAT, NO PROBLEM

When I was young and fresh out of school
I wondered, what with my life, would I do;
Then suddenly, it occurred to me-
Why not join the Navy and put out to sea.

The joys of traveling this marvelous world,
Endless adventures would certainly unfurl;
So I found a recruiter and signed on the line;
Now with the fear of 'boot camp' on my mind.

For I entered camp not knowing how to swim,
Making my chances of passing mighty slim.
I'd jump in the pool and sink straight to the bottom,
I'd feel an arm, then hear 'I've got him'.

These failures continued throughout boot camp,
Till it finally came down to my very last chance;
Once again I sank and was again pulled out,
Time to meet the captain, there was little doubt.

"I've been observing your attempts to float
My advice to you - stay away from boats;
Yet if in the Navy, you still want to be-
There's a way in which you may still go to sea.

If ever you become lost to your ship
Heed these mandatory orders that I now give;
Sink rapidly to the ocean floor
And run like hell to the lands dry shores!"

"Captain Sir, I'll do you one better --
For when disaster's storm clouds start to gather;
I'll need to be assigned to a submarine,
Where I'd still be at sea fulfilling my dreams.

For a submarine resides below the brine,
There'd be no sinking or floating of any kind;
I'd already be near the ocean floor-
I'd just open the hatch and run for shore!!"

G.Q. IN V-4 DIVISION

Intrepid were those 'Grape Apes'
J.P. Purple, flowed their blood;
Awaiting the returning birds,
In formation, high above.

Lying on the deck in pseudo- sleep,
The likes of which was shallow;
The thunder of the forward cats,
Meant recovery, soon would follow.

Our dungarees were fuel- soaked;
Our bodies sore and sleep deprived;
Engaged in 'General Quarters'
Yet our spirit still survived.

The pattern of launch and recovery,
Continuously around the clock;
Each plane fueled and quickly staged,
With the removal of the chocks.

Finally, that glorious moment
When that last bird caught the cable;
The steam died from the catapults
And all planes were in the stable.

At last, we removed our headgear,
Our goggles, gloves and ground wires;
To hit the shower and our racks
Was now our only genuine desire!

SCUTTLED

In the silent darkness of the deep;
In the locker of eternal sleep;
Scuttled and forever destined,
To remain eternally where she's resting.

Fathoms below the sunlit surface;
An unseen epitaph to the purpose,
Of this worthy ship and valiant crew,
Serving the U.S. Navy, proud and true.

From 'The Med' to the Indian Ocean;
From The Captain to junior bosun (boatswain)
O'er thirty years they served this nation,
Carrying out duties without hesitation.

However, ships and crews do not last forever,
Old ships rust and crews grow older;
Crews retire and move on with their lives,
While old ships, live on, only in the archives.

This was the fate of C.V. sixty-six,
Led out to sea then quickly deep-sixed;
The 'AMERICA': this grand old vessel,
Will rust on the sea floor, now and forever!

HOW SAD!!!

CHAPTER FIVE

FAITH

NO FEAR OF DEATH

Every living soul on the Earth,
Must face the certainty of death
And of the unknown- what's to come
After they've taken their last breath.

Will they ferry 'cross the River Styx
With Charon as their ferryman;
Or will they be cast into Hell,
To spend eternity with Satan?

Or will they walk toward a light
And follow it to who knows where;
Or be placed in some dark hole,
Their existence completed there?

THANK GOD! I have no fear of death,
For I believe in JESUS CHRIST!
I'll dwell with my lord in heaven,
For I'm promised eternal life!!

AMEN!!

Frankie Blodgett

SUNDAY CONFUSION

'Twas the day before tomorrow
I remember it very well
Seems like only yesterday
But with time, it's hard to tell.

I set out on a mission
Or did I stay at home?
The car is in the driveway
I guess I didn't roam.

I arose to serve my savior
At least that's what I said
I guess I must have faltered
For here I am, still in bed.

DEEPEST SPACE

We all have an inner space
Which is just inside our outer space
An area which we call our own.
However all throughout our outer space
Which is just outside our inner space
Lies an evil world, we can't atone.

Now incasing our inner space
Which is just inside our outer space
Our physical brain is what we find.
And just within our physical brain
Which is just inside our outer space
Is that which we refer to as our mind.

Now there exists a deeper space
Which is just inside our inner space
That which we refer to as our soul.
Which is just inside our inner space
Which is just inside our outer space
To protect it from all evil is our goal.

Now far above our outer space
And far above our inner space
Our Great GOD on high doth seek
He seekest not our outer space
He seekest not our inner space
He seeks our deepest space, our soul to keep!

ONLY GOD

I sometimes truly become discouraged
Seeing how despicable mankind has become;
It is then, I turn my eyes skyward
And realize what Natures God has done!

The ageless stars, high in the heavens
Appear exactly as in my youth,
When dad and I gazed skyward;
Truly one of life's stable truths.

Sadly, my dad has long since departed
And life on Earth is in malefic change;
Yet those glorious stars still twinkle
And the constellations still remain.

Regardless of the petty changes,
Mankind may inflict upon the Earth;
Only God can move the ageless stars
And truly change the Universe!!

TURN RIGHT OR ANNIHILATION

A relatively minute object
Crossed the Earth's orbital plane;
Be it: asteroid or comet;
The result remains the same.

How unfortunate was the timing,
As to the Earths point in revolution;
For to prevent man's total annihilation,
Scientists had no effectual solution.

Mankind was morally spiraling downward
And had turned away from God;
This was an extremely dangerous course,
That man had chosen to trod.

For the impact was devastating;
Extinction being the end result.
A power far greater than that of man,
Brought his sinful reign to a halt!

Frankie Blodgett

BELIEVE

Can it be: catastrophe?
Present in the here and now;
The signs apparent,
Of a society errant;
God's word, they, disavow.

Can't they see: instability?
In the lifestyles they have chosen;
Their sinful lives,
Have caused great strife;
Their cold hearts forever frozen.

Only Gods pure love, from up above,
Can save them from the fire;
Believing: John 3:16,
Can come between,
Eternal Hell or singing in Heaven's choir!

HERE TODAY

That which is
Is that which was
GOD is all
And always was.

The Universe is infinite
Time goes on
Today mankind is here
Tomorrow gone.

Frankie Blodgett

SAVING LIGHTS

It was the summer of sixty-eight,
The hour was early, yet I was late;
The wind was still, the humidity high,
Thus a heavy fog, yet no alibi.

For I was light keeper, out on the ledge,
To faithfully serve, I'd taken the pledge;
I'd rowed to the mainland for provisions,
Now six miles back in these conditions.

The mist was thick, visibility zero;
Bound by duty, certainly no hero;
I knew the bearing back to the rock;
With oars in hand and compass in box.

The first couple of miles was unnerving;
Trying to hold course, needle swerving;
Finally a faint glint of flashing light,
From the first order Fresnel piercing the night.

Guided back by the towers saving light,
Kept by my assistant, throughout the night;
With ebb tide at keel and favorable winds,
The light had guided me safely home again.

For when I'm lost on life's foggy seas,
Confused and bewildered, GOD provides a lee.
Just as a keeper is guided by his light;
GOD is my beacon, shining through life's dark nights!

CHAPTER SIX

FREE SPIRIT

FREE SPIRIT

Freedom is a glorious state
Far above the bonds of man,
She floats upon the wings of the wind
And never makes a plan.

As the riptide draws the soul from shore,
A counter course there must be,
To ride the mighty surf ashore
And set the spirit free.

The vastness of the heavens
Extend for evermore;
The harmony of void and stars
Is too great to be ignored.

So wander, oh free spirit!
The Universe lies ahead:
You'll live a greater adventure;
Than found in any book you've ever read!

Frankie Blodgett

A SIMPLE MAN'S PARADISE

Sitting 'neath a gumbo limbo,
Sea grapes hanging all around;
Sunshine shimmering on the bay,
A cool breeze coming off the sound.

Filling pits on a Mancala Board
With nicker beans from a gourd;
Just a 'counting and a capturing',
Drinking rum as fast as poured.

On this timeless isolated beach,
An old native sitting across the board,
Fretting o'er his captured beans,
Losing more than he can afford.

The vivid green sea gleams before me,
The brilliant blue sky wide above,
An amusing old stork, to my right,
To my left, a gentle pair of dove.

Others rave about the tropics'
Grand hotels with lovely courts,
Luxury suits, pools and saunas
And entertainment of all sorts.

To me, life must be kept simple
With no worry, stress or haste;
To live in any alternate manner
Is honestly, such a waste!

OLD GLORY

Thirteen ribbons in the wind,
This is how it all began
Seven of red, six of white;
The thirteen colonies did unite.

The crown had stolen our fathers' freedoms;
Independence had become the reason,
To fight for all that we hold dear
And keep our freedoms, throughout the years.

Fifty white stars, on a field of blue;
This is how our nation grew;
From thirteen colonies to fifty states;
All have made this nation great.

Combined, we have 'THE STARS AND STRIPES'
A symbol of our protected rights;
'OLD GLORY', may she forever fly
And may our nation, never die!!

Frankie Blodgett

CHAPTER SEVEN

WINDS OF CHANGE

PATRIOTIC HOPE

Each day as I gaze out from my window
A golden eagle greets my stare,
Perched high upon my flagpole;
At its feet, the focus of my prayers.

A simple rectangular piece of fabric
Displaying the colors, red white and blue,
Still proudly waving inspirationally
O'er the land of the free and the true.

However, complete despair overwhelms me
As I scrutinize the leaders we chose;
Their policies are corrupt and self-serving
And their ideologies are enabling our foes.

Their goal is for a much larger government,
Placing themselves in ever increasing control;
Destroying the constitutional guidelines,
Diluting the Republic, which we know.

My prayers are for infinite wisdom
On our leaders be ethically endowed;
And bestow in them a steadfast courage,
T'would have made our founding fathers proud.

For 'THE CONSTITUTION' is our nations anchor!
Guaranteeing the liberties and rights, we hold dear.
May, 'WE The People' always control our government
And avoid the trans-patriotism, our forefathers feared.

WINDS OF CHANGE

An arrogant leader, with a corrupt agenda;
The naive did proclaim their king
For clueless men in a dog eat dog world,
Is a recipe for long pig.

Trust not he with a silvery tongue
For a blackheart is its mate;
A waggin' tongue runs as a striking asp,
Spewing the venom of deceit and hate!

The winds of change blew rapidly;
The future seemed cold and gray,
The wisdom of o'er two hundred years,
Was so suddenly stripped away.

A people led to total ruin,
Through the treachery of a few,
Whose deceptive philosophies,
The populace never knew.

The silence of a nation
Now weeping for that which was;
Once clueless to his vile scheme;
Caught up in all the buzz.

The power of false rhetoric,
The oblivious did believe;
So enthralled in all the hype,
Were the gullible and naive.

His unscrupulous plan was simple;
Class warfare his calculated theme;
Aided with a far left media,
Spelled the end of the 'AMERICAN DREAM'

History will long remember,
The destruction of the great;
The death of FREE AMERICA,
The consequence of lies and hate!!!

DESPERATION TO REMAIN FREE

It had never been our plan
Of throwing crap into the fan;
Yet then again the time was right,
To recite dirges through the night.

Sorrow! Sorrow! For our nation;
Cries and pleas for resuscitation;
All of which fell upon deaf ears;
We're drowning in a sea of fear.

A bell is tolling in the tower,
Signifying, lateness of the hour:
Action! Action! The only course,
We must sadly mount the horse.

With an outcome this uncertain;
With disaster we are flirting;
Yet to do nothing, all is lost;
For it's a no win coin toss.

Still all the hopes and all the fears,
Gathered for o'er two hundred years,
Teeter upon fates pointed summit;
Thus, we must battle or we'll plummet!

Onward! Onward! Into battle,
Must not let our armor rattle;
We must charge with steady lance,
For there shall be no second chance!

MOCCASIN IN OUR BOAT

When I was young
And rather irresponsible,
My poor judgment
Put my friend in the hospital.

I had a good friend
Who was terrified of spiders;
He always referred to them,
'Those nasty little biters'.

When we'd go fishing
In our small boat,
I'd run him through webs
Just to get his goat.

One damp morn I spied
A dew covered web,
Motored on over
Until it was on his head.

He yelled and swung wildly
Till his pole struck a branch,
Knocking a moccasin into the boat-
He never stood a chance.

Frankie Blodgett

For a moccasin
Is an aggressive snake,
Extremely dangerous
And full of hate.

Now I'm older
Yet none the wiser,
I run through life,
Still motoring toward spiders.

I run with the left
Never thinking or caring,
Believing the drive-bys
And the bull they're sharing.

The LOW INFORMATION label
Sure fits me well,
For I'm voting my country
Straight to HELL!

I never actually realized
The importance of my vote;
Now look what I've done-
I've help put a moccasin in our boat!!

NEW SNOW ON THE HILL

In early November
Every two years or so,
'The Hill' is covered
With a pure virgin snow.

The rejuvenating flakes
Softly blanket the ground;
A refreshing new spirit
Is suddenly found.

An awakening of hope,
The snow's purity brings;
Somewhat like the joy
That one feels in The Spring

The moon on the monument,
A long shadow does cast,
Upon the face of the snow;
A dark reminder of the past.

For the embedded filth
In the cold earth below,
Does forge slowly upward
And corrupts the pure snow.

Frankie Blodgett

And from the atmosphere
Smoke and dust does descend,
Thus subverting the snow;
Just how much, does depend--

On the amount of contact
With the underlying green
And the nature of the snow's
Ability to remain clean.

Yet e'er in the end,
There is one thing cocksure;
Near the embedded filth
No purity can endure.

The pulse of 'The Hill'
Is rooted in green;
Sadly in retrospect,
Purity couldn't succeed!

Dolefully, the 'Spring of Hope'
Must be prolonged with a tear,
For real hope dims greatly
With each slowly passing year.

VORTEX

The monstrous winds tore at the ever helpless sails,
Ripping them angrily from their failing riggings;
As tumultuous waves bashed the fore mast,
Splintering it as if it were but a sapling.

The savage wind, a great counter flow did create,
Generating, what began as a small whirlpool,
E'er enlarging into an enormous maelstrom;
With no escape, its lifeline was ripped from the spool.

Some centuries later, a huge ill-fated star,
Afloat in a sea of infinite time and space,
Found itself captured by a massive black hole,
From whose gravitational field, there was no escape.

Spinning e'er faster toward the crushing vortex-
Of gravity, created by a massive neutron star;
For once it entered the event horizon
It was past the point of no return, it had gone too far.

Currently, America is on the verge of death;
Our great nation, however perilously she spins
Through the Ergo sphere of political destruction,
With a freedom killing vortex e'er closing-in

CHAPTER EIGHT

---◦◦◦—◄█►—◦◦◦---

PIPING ME HOME

KEEPERS OF THE EARTH

They are the 'Keepers of the Earth',
Standing sentry since her birth;
Traveling between unknown dimensions,
Staunch overseers of man's intentions.

They walk the Earth in secret numbers;
Timeless sentinels o'er natures wonders;
Their mournful cries ride the wind,
Concern for a world, they cannot mend.

Although their sightings are quite common,
Solid proof has never been gotten;
Scattered footprints are all they leave;
It's no wonder, so few believe.

Silent watchmen who deplore us,
Peering from the deepest forests,
Bewailing o'er the wounded Earth,
From their lofty mountain perch.

Waiting for the inevitable time,
When man will cross that sacred line;
They'll then unleash all Natures force;
Man's annihilation will take its course!

They are Sasquatch! They are Yeti!
Around the world, their names are many;
Primal entities, who were the first;
They are the 'Keepers of the Earth'!

BEGONE FOREST NYMPH

Be gone! Enchanting forest nymph,
For man is destroying your forests;
Turn a deaf ear, pretend not to hear
His chainsaw's agonizing chorus.

Flee quickly! Let your eyes not see;
Gone are your colonnades of wood;
Now only slash debris remains,
Where once your lovely forests stood.

Levelled, are your hinterlands;
Once so timeless and serene;
Gone is the glorious wildlife,
Where in forests, once it teamed.

But there's an interconnectedness,
Binding all life upon this sphere;
Fair nymph, when man destroys your forests;
Wasteful mankind will also disappear!

THE DRY LAKE BED

Anguish o'er the imperiled lake,
Its arid state conveys heartache;
This wretched drought, beauty slayer;
Sorrow not unlike a sea less sailor.

Standing spellbound with vexing heart
In a dry bed, once a work of art;
With e'er flowing tears raising dust;
For a watery bed, my eyes did lust.

Frankie Blodgett

The rising heat from the dry ole lake;
A delusional image did create;
A mirage offering vain desire
And still it set my heart on fire.

Yet, nature has a primal resilience
To naturally restore its original brilliance;
Thus each morn, I wake up hoping:
Great God, with rain, his heavens he'll open!

REST IN THE MIST

The sun was slowly rising,
O'er the blue and tranquil sea;
A thick cloud bank was approaching;
Completely surrounding me.

Enveloped in a misty cloud,
Masking the maddening would outside;
A silent world, without the crowds;
A place where my soul could hide.

The only sounds to be heard,
Was the slapping of the sea
And the trill cry of a sea bird;
My spirit felt totally free.

The insanity of the modern world,
Was obscured for just a rest;
A few moments without a spoken word;
This solitude, I caressed.

But the mist would soon be flying;
The sun would rapidly burn through;
The tranquility would be dying;
A sad return to the busy world, I knew!

Frankie Blodgett

CRY FOR THE HUMAN RACE

Listen to the 'GOD OF NATURE'
The message is simple and pure,
Be as one with earth and sea
And hold the Earth forever dear.

Gaze upon the mighty sea:
Feel the earth beneath your feet;
Listen to the 'Song of Life'
Then life's treasures you shall reap.

Your mind is but a gossamer
Floating whimsically about,
In a timeless peaceful trance,
Free of nebulosity and doubt.

Yet, man has profaned the sacred Earth,
Through destruction and careless waste;
The death of the Earth, is the death of man;
Cry deeply for the human race!

REFLECT IN THE FOREST

Fear not the forest
Where life sings in chorus,
Where serenity's found
And nature abounds.

Fear not the shade
For it's out in the glade,
Where human demons dance
In deep worldly trance.

Not all's as it seems,
Reality and dreams;
Black appears white;
Wrong appears right.

An errant society;
No hope for sobriety;
Fumbles about,
Always missing out,

On that which is pure
And naturally sincere.
So to the forest return;
To satisfy your yearn.

In the shadows reflect,
Where your soul can connect
With all that is pure
And with all you hold dear.

Frankie Blodgett

SOJOURN INTO SILENCE

During moments of restful leisure,
When peaceful silence rules the hour;
I often reflect, in the stillness,
Inducing meditative powers.

Shadowy thoughts becoming wordless;
Complex ideas suddenly clear.
A juvenescence of cognition;
Miraculous insight without fear.

Free from radio and television,
Away from computers and cell phones;
Free of laughter and conversation,
Cherishing the silence of alone.

However these sojourns into silence,
Are just that, a temporary trip;
Silence and alone, soon become lonesome;
For the human spirit needs fellowship.

PROGRESSION

PRIMO

GENESIS

THE PRIMORDIAL STEW

ALL THAT LIVES

BEGAN IN THAT BREW

MICROBES

INVERTEBRATES

FISH RULED THE SEA

AMPHIBIANS CAME ASHORE

REPTILES EXCEED

DINOSAURS

ASTEROIDS

MAMMALS TOOK CONTROL

MAN RULED THE EARTH

TIL HE LET GO

COMPUTERS

ROBOTICS

ARTIFICIAL LIFE

ALL NOW SYNTHETIC

THE END OF BIO- STRIFE!!!

THE SAME OLD SONG

Upon Earth we dwell
Between Heaven and Hell
In a limbo, that is life;
We sing so strong
The same old song,
The song of love and strife.

From our birth
Upon the Earth
Contradictions do persist;
To kill is wrong,
The same old song,
We must kill, just to exist.

We fight to live,
Yet time's a sieve,
Life filters down through time;
We laugh and cry
As time flies by
For life turns upon a dime.

Life is a folly,
Yet melancholy
And oh, so very trivial;
Life or death,
A screwed-up mess,
Each choice is ever pivotal.

Frankie Blodgett

For those who share
The daily fare
The drudgery, that is life;
We moil along
The same old song
A life of toil and strife.

We sing a dirge
We cannot purge
Which echoes within our minds;
A song of sorrow
Through eternal tomorrows,
Seeking answers we can't find.

Yet there's a cure
For death is sure
To conquer everyone;
We sing along
The same old song
Till our work on Earth is done.

When our race has been run
Another has begun,
Someone has filled our slot;
Right or wrong
The same old song,
Succession matters not!

FALLEN FROM THE TIMELINE

I was moving toward the future,
Smoothly gliding with the rest;
Heading toward my 'Golden Years'
Looking forward to life's best.

When I tripped upon the present,
Rapidly fell into the past,
Watched the future pass me by
And it all happened in a flash.

I had fallen from the time line;
The future didn't seem to fit,
In a world of modern gadgets;
I just couldn't find my niche.

The past was what I longed for,
A much slower pace of life;
A friendly hometown people,
A world with much less strife.

My life is in the good ole past,
Ne'er made it o'er that futuristic hump:
For you see, I've fallen from the time line
And I simply can't get up!

WINDS OF TIME

Soulful spirits of life so pure,
Bound in time, throughout the years;
In a never ending cosmic dash
Through the future and the past.

The cycle of time is but a blur
As through time and space, the Earth is hurled;
Stars and galaxies streak ever by
As if meteors in an Earthly sky.

With no beginning and no end,
Certain Physics laws are forbidden to men;
Past to future, future is past-
General Physics is put to task.

We recognize things which we never knew,
With so many occurrences of Deja vu;
For most remembrances of past lives-
Are blown away by the 'Winds of time'.

Yet memories caught in the fabric of space,
That the time somehow failed to erase,
Strike a receptor in the mind
And somehow avoid the 'Winds of Time'.

MIRROR OF TIME

The mirror of time
Reflects my life,
It matters not
Whether wrong or right.

The true image
Of my past,
The shadows of time
Which couldn't last.

If I could pick
One point in time
And travel back
Within my mind;

It would be
Early in my youth
When life was easy
And innocence ruled.

CYCLE OF LIFE

I see a light,
I yell- Oh Hell!
`For it's too late
To turn back now,

I've been slapped,
I suddenly cry,
Voices cheer,
I wonder why.

I race through life
For several years,
With many joys
And far more tears.

Then suddenly
The light is gone,
Leaving me wondering-
What went wrong?

I grope about
In the black,
I feel a push,
I feel a slap.

I see a light,
I yell- Oh Hell!
For it's too late,
To turn back now!

BLACK BOG

How lonely is the fog
Which shrouds the ole 'BLACK BOG',
Its deep blue vapors seem
To have destroyed all my dreams.

How black is the water
As aimlessly it maunders,
Moving slowly in time
Through the canyons of my mind.

No sunlight invades
The bogs impenetrable shade;
How utterly dark is my way,
Not a single sun lit ray.

All of life's joys are gone,
Since I've become a pawn;
My life is in regression;
IN this bog known as: DEPRESSION!!!!

ICE BOUND- NO MORE

The ice, which is life
Within me melts,
Creating fear
And causing doubt.

This frozen existence
To which I cling,
Imprisons my spirit
And clips my wings.

To repel the cold,
I actually live;
Freedoms hope,
The heat doth give.

Alas! I finally
Gave up the ghost;
Departed the ice
Which was my host.

My loosened soul
Has taken wing;
A spirit free; now
Thru the Universe sings!

THE FINAL DECISION

The old bo'sum (boatswain) jumped from his rack
Uniformed up and sadly left his quarters
Then down the passageway to the ladder
Knowing that he must carry out his orders.

A cold north blow quickly greeted him
As he stepped out onto the deck;
His old eyes watered from the cold
As they made their final inspect.

He turned his pea coat collar up,
Hoisted his sea bag from the deck,
Saluted the ensign one last time
And departed upon his final brow trek.

For he was being put ashore this day,
Being relieved by a raw green boot,
A pollywog who'd ne'er crossed the line
Or rounded the horn; an anchor without a fluke.

His entire life had been spent a sea;
Land had always been an unfit place to dwell,
A place for leave and liberty;
Otherwise a dry prison like hell'

Although his new duty station was far inland;
The seas pull held to the coast:
Deep in thought, he walked the beach for miles
Looking as if he'd seen a ghost.

He suddenly stopped and looked seaward;
A contented happiness filled his face,
He now knew he'd discovered his destiny
And that he'd run his final race.

He turned and walked beneath the brine;
Life had called in his final marker;
For the sea had brought him eternally home
To join his comrades of the locker!

PREDETERMINED FATE

The primal fire of life,
The grand creator of all,
Architect of time,
Determines all to befall.

The fire: the father.
The mother of life;
Sends her smoke upward,
E'er attaining new heights.

The smoke vibrantly dances
As it rises from the flames;
Forming swirling shafts;
Streaming upward untamed.

Only to be dispersed,
By a calculated breeze;
A very brief sojourn;
Destroyed with ease.

Such is the destiny
Of life's colonnade;
The breezes of time
Approach and invade.

For time conquers all;
There is no escape.
The dispersal: the death:
A predetermined fate!!

Frankie Blodgett

PIPING ME HOME

Lost in a world which had left me behind,
For the good old days, I did languish and pine;
I dropped to my knees and prayed above,
I might again spin yarns of the sea, I love.

I guess that great GOD heard my pleas
For I heard the locker callin' to me;
I feebly arose from my knees
And hobbled down to my beloved sea.

On a strange dark and moonless night,
In a windless black, e'er so quiet,
The sea before me lie near still,
A flat ebb tide with motion nil.

From somewhere out in the boundless sea,
A faint call awoke a memory;
Whence so e'er this heartfelt summons-
On the wings of death, it was comin'

Piper of pleasure; piper of pain,
Spinner of years; memory's flame.
The sea is beckoning, The Reaper near;
I'm going home and have no fear!

With brittle body and dulling mind,
A merry yarn, would do me fine;
Sharing sea stories 'neath the briny foam,
For an old bo'sum (boatswain) is 'PIPING ME HOME'!

CHAPTER NINE

JUST FOR FUN

BUGBEAR MOUNTAIN

Deep in the sylvan backwoods
Where folklore is understood
To tell of dark realities
And lost secrets of the wood.

Therein stands a mysterious mountain;
The fabled, 'OLE BUGBEAR'
A supernatural haven,
Few ever venture there.

A land of trolls and goblins
Of specter and of sprite
Of ghouls and horrid monsters
And vampires of the night.

Near the snowline of this mountain,
Alongside a babbling pristine stream,
Sets a cozy little cabin,
In the most solitude of scenes.

This cabin's been my home
For nigh long sixty years;
Ever since I told those tales,
Which started all the fear.

Now my yarns have grown to legends,
Commonly believed throughout the land;
Hence, I've lived a quiet peaceful life,
Alone, here in this monster-free hinterland.

THE ULTIMATE HUNT

The moon had an eerie sullen glow
As we emerged from the hunting lodge,
We had come so very far
Me and my buddy Sarge.

We had dreamed for so many years
Of coming to this hunting ground;
For it was well documented, to contain;
The best game that could be found.

I remember my father's photos
And the tales, that he did share,
Of how he shot this creature,
More cunning than Neyak or bear.

Now, these creatures are fairly intelligent,
For animals so poorly evolved
And their meat is extremely tasty,
If field dressed, immediately when felled.

The hunt was extremely exciting,
Enhancing the rush and the thrill;
With a creature so elusive and cleaver;
Climaxed by the conquest and kill.

This evening as we sat 'round our fire;
With our glorious kill, serving as our feast;
We raved of our extraordinary hunt,
And our conquest o'er this beast.

For today was truly our greatest day,
Two Zurites, from the Planet NuBreene .
For today was the day, we traveled to Earth
And killed our first Human Being!!

NO BACKING A TENT

Left the RV dealership
With my new fifth wheel,
Was extremely pleased
For I received a great deal.

I drove very carefully
Until I learned the score,
For never in my life
Had I towed before.

I made it to the campground,
Quite alright
And pulled head first
Right into my site.

Frankie Blodgett

I suddenly realized
That I had made a mistake
For I was facing a tree
And I couldn't escape.

I couldn't pull forward,
I couldn't go back,
For the basic skill of backing
I did lack.

To return to the street,
I was sure eager;
However, I had no knowledge
Of the proper procedure.

So I turned the wheel
Hard to the right;
In the blink of an eye
My rig jackknifed.

This continued for
What seemed like hours;
Apparently this task
Was beyond my powers.

Well, I turned the wheel
Every way but loose;
I finally realized
That it was no use.

Fussin' and cussun'
My anger, I did vent;
I left the rig right there;
Went out and bought a TENT!!

SCRAWLIN' POULTRY
IN DA SWAMP

I once were scrawlin 'poultry
Down yonder in the fen
Ad a brown bag an crayon
Ad no papier or ink pen.

Neath a lonely cypress
Ma backside on a knee
Hung an orery mocsun
Way bove me in dat tree.

Ma feet was in da wadder
Of dat muddy ole swamp
A gater slid on at me
Fixin ta do da swamp chomp.

Didn't scare me none cept one thang
I ad on ma bran new crocs
Ifin ole gater bit ma tows-
Eed also get ma sox.

Ma mama would be afussin
Ma paw would tan ma hide
I reccond'd I shoe'd do sumptin'
Ta sav ma Sudern Pride.

So I kicked dat dern gater
Wight in is toofy snoot
E flew off a mite fur peasee
Steel toad crocs is likea boot.

Den I reached-up in dat tree
N grab da dern ole snake
I ad im round da nek
N flung im in da lake.

Den got bak ta ma poultry
Tryin ta scrawl a lit'l verse
But ifin ya thank ma words is bad
Ma poultry is a derncite worse!

THE REJUVENATION MACHINE

Scientists have been working
For years in their labs
On a marvelous machine
That turns men into lads.

A machine that fills men
With wonder and joy,
A magic machine
That turns men into boys.

A machine that adds
Spirit and life to one's heart,
Which lightens the soul
The moment it starts.

A machine that invigorates
And revs-up the brain;
A machine which rejuvenates
And rekindles life's flame.

Scientists had struggled
Years, to come up with a name,
But all the great words
Were simply too plain.

Finally they discovered
A word that just stuck:
Why don't we call it?
'THE PICKUP TRUCK'

UNCONCERNED

I remember much less
Than I've forgot
Feeling forlorn
Yet caring hot.

I still probably know more
Than I've ever learned
Feeling confused
Yet not concerned.

BEWARE OF THE DRINKING WATER

Microbes, bacteria and protozoa- OH MY!
Through my microscope- I do spy!
Each water droplet teeming with life,
How can so many organisms simultaneously survive?

Mitosis and other simple reproduction,
Rapid replications and reductions;
Continually feeding and dividing,
Increasing in number and surviving.

Euglena, whipping about with their flagellum,
Circling the droplet like Magellan;
Paramecium with its oral groove,
Continually moving, taking in food.

Amoeba with its pseudopodia,
Another example of Protozoa,
Changing shape, surrounding their prey;
Eating, excreting and mixing in the fray.

So before you sip another water drop,
It might be wise if you'd just stop,
And think of all the organisms that would cheer-
If you would switch and grab a BEER!

Frankie Blodgett

MELODIOUS REBIRTH

Light years away, on a young world unknown,
Soon will occur a miracle full blown;
Life as we know it will again resume,
At 'The Gathering' of life's melodies and tunes.

Trillions of melodies lost in time;
Tunes which were lived with purpose and rhyme,
Are deeply woven within the fabric of space;
Carefully preserved for the next- 'Human Race'.

For music is the universal code;
Delicately replicated as each soul implodes.
Vitals of life transported on notes,
Containing all of man's fears and all of his hopes.

All that man is and all that man was,
Everything man will do and all that he does;
Is carefully encoded upon each melodious wave;
Ensuring that his essence will always be saved.

Soon, all the notes will converge at one place,
At a designated point in time and in space;
The 'Human Race' will experience a fantastic rebirth;
In the oddest of places- a small planet called EARTH!

'TWAS AN ANT THAT DID ME IN

'Twas an ant that did me in;
I found some days you just can't win;
I was out walking with my mutt,
When an ole ant bit my butt'

My old dog rolled and laughed,
As I flew rapidly from my pants,
I was in such a dad-blamed rush
I tripped and fell into the brush.

I just couldn't seem to catch a break,
For I landed on a darn ole snake
I then became quite alarmed,
When his poison fangs sank into my arm.

As I jumped up and quickly fled,
A tree branch hit me in the head;
Dazed, I didn't see that hog,
Charging wildly from the bog.

All I remember are those tusks;
As into shock, I deeply rushed;
Yet somehow, I did survive,
And even managed to stay alive.

Yet honestly, in retrospect;
As my thoughts, I now collect
So now the blame, I have to pin-
'Twas an ant that did me in!

　Frankie Blodgett

FLOATED UPON THE SWELLS

Once I floated upon the seas ever rolling swells
Which push forever toward life's eternal saving shore,
Listening to the solemn tales, the sea so often tells

Far landward, near the beach, the breakers forever roar
Spawning spindrift from the seas perpetual womb,
As so highly above the cadenced waves it soars.

Rising up and falling back, in a sallied swoon;
Fainting and groping the helpless eroding sand,
Continually aided by the ever pulling moon.

Until my aching body, upon the beach did lie,
Abandoned by the constant seas ever rolling swells;
Then suddenly lying breathless, my lips released a sigh.

Longingly my heart beats wildly, for a tale I must tell,
Of when I floated helplessly upon the seas e'er rolling
swells.

ABOUT THE AUTHOR

The author's life began in rural upstate New York where he resided in the small village of Chenango Forks. At a very young age, he developed a deep interest and an appreciation of nature. The Chenango River became the focus of his early years. Then in his early teens he moved with his family to N.E. Florida and instantly fell in love with the Atlantic Ocean, its tributaries and coastline. For the rest of his life boating, fishing and studying sea life were a major part of his life. Then after graduating from high school he joined U.S. Navy where his duties were to fuel planes on the flight deck of aircraft carriers. It was in this phase of his life, while traveling to other countries, that he truly realized how special AMERICA really is! He also understood that it is our Constitution which separates us from the rest of the world and makes our republic GREAT!! After his tour of duty in the Navy, he attended Jacksonville University on the G.I.Bill. He spent the rest of his life believing that the love of God, Country and Family coupled with hard work, honesty and the liberties and protections assured us in the U.S. Constitution are the reasons this land has been so blessed!